Searchlight
BOOKS™

Climate Change WITHDRAWN

Climate Change and
Energy Technology

Rebecca E. Hirsch

Lerner Publications ◆ Minneapolis

Lerner Publications Company
A division of Lerner Publishing Group, Inc.
241 First Avenue North
Minneapolis, MN 55401 USA

For reading levels and more information, look up this title at www.lernerbooks.com.

Main body text set in Adrianna Regular 14/20.
Typeface provided by Chank.

Library of Congress Cataloging-in-Publication Data

Names: Hirsch, Rebecca E., author.
Title: Climate change and energy technology / Rebecca E. Hirsch.
Description: Minneapolis : Lerner Publications, [2019] | Series: Searchlight books.
    Climate change | Audience: Age 8–11. | Audience: Grade 4 to 6. | Includes
    bibliographical references and index.
Identifiers: LCCN 2018015744 (print) | LCCN 2018026400 (ebook) |
    ISBN 9781541543652 (eb pdf) | ISBN 9781541538665 (lb : alk. paper) |
    ISBN 9781541545908 (pb : alk. paper)
Subjects: LCSH: Energy conservation—Juvenile literature. | Climatic changes—Juvenile
    literature. | Green technology—Juvenile literature.
Classification: LCC TJ163.35 (ebook) | LCC TJ163.35 .H57 2019 (print) |
    DDC 621.042028/6—dc23

LC record available at https://lccn.loc.gov/2018015744

Manufactured in the United States of America
1-45049-35876-6/12/2018

Contents

Chapter 1

WHAT IS CLIMATE CHANGE?

Look outside. What is the weather like today? Weather changes from day to day. Some days are warm, and some are cold.

Climate is the usual weather for a place. For example, some places are warm in summer but cold in winter. Earth's climate is the climate of the whole planet. It's what you get when you add up all the different climates around the world.

Rain is a type of weather. Some places have a rainy climate, while others have rain only occasionally.

This illustration shows the ice age, a time period in the past when Earth was much colder than it is in modern times.

Just as weather can change, so can climate. Weather can change quickly, but it takes a long time for climate to change. Climate change takes hundreds or thousands of years.

Through Earth's history, the climate has changed many times. At times in the past, Earth was warmer. At other times, it was colder. These warm and cold periods lasted for thousands or even millions of years.

Earth's Fever

Scientists tell us Earth's climate is changing again. This time the climate is growing warmer. The planet's temperature has gone up a little more than 1°F (0.6°C) over the past hundred years.

Scientists say Earth will keep growing warmer over the next hundred years. The extra heat will cause rising seas, flooding, droughts, and severe weather.

A warming climate can mean more extreme storms of all kinds—even blizzards.

Cutting down forests contributes to climate change. Without trees to soak up carbon dioxide, more of the gas builds up in the atmosphere.

In the past, Earth's climate changed because of natural events. Sometimes the sun would send out more or less energy. Sometimes a volcano would erupt, and that would change the climate.

But this time is different. Human activity is changing the climate. Riding in cars, turning on lights, and heating and cooling our homes all contribute to climate change. These activities require the burning of fossil fuels such as coal, natural gas, and oil. Burning these fuels has a big effect on the planet's climate.

Chapter 2

CLIMATE AND ENERGY

In the United States, 39 percent of the electricity we use comes from coal burned in a power plant.

When you flip on a light switch, where does the electricity come from? In the United States, the electricity usually comes from a power plant.

The electricity travels through power lines to reach our homes. We use this electricity when we flip on a light switch, power up a computer, or cook our food.

Fossil fuels were formed from the ancient remains of plants and animals. Heat and pressure from being buried under rocks converted the remains to coal, oil, and gas.

Many power plants burn coal or natural gas to make electricity. These fossil fuels were formed millions of years ago. When we use them up, they can't be replaced.

Burning fossil fuels releases carbon dioxide into the air. This invisible gas traps heat, causing the air to heat up. Having too much carbon dioxide in the atmosphere is a cause of climate change.

EVERY DAY, THE SUN RELEASES TEN THOUSAND TIMES THE WORLD'S TOTAL ENERGY USE. SCIENTISTS ARE LOOKING FOR MORE EFFICIENT WAYS TO HARNESS THAT ENERGY.

Wind and Sun

The wind and sun are renewable sources of energy. These sources naturally replenish themselves. They don't produce carbon dioxide or add to climate change.

Solar power is electricity made from the sun. Solar cells turn sunlight into electricity. A solar panel, which contains many solar cells, can be installed on a rooftop to provide electricity for a building.

Large collections of solar cells can run a power plant. Solar power plants can produce electricity for thousands of homes.

This solar power plant in Mexico covers an area the size of forty football fields.

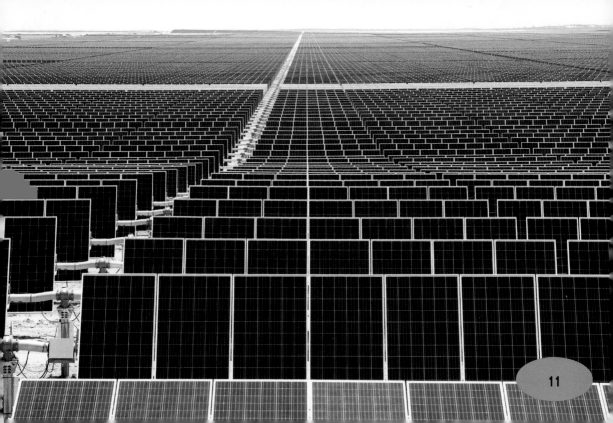

Another way people use solar power is in thermal power plants. Large, curved mirrors reflect sunlight toward a receiver. The energy from the sunlight then heats water and makes steam. The steam powers a turbine.

A turbine is a machine with blades that spin around. It takes energy in water, steam, or air and helps turn it into electricity.

Wind can also make electricity. We capture the wind's energy with wind turbines. The blades of a wind turbine spin in the wind. The blades connect to a generator that produces electricity.

Wind farms are collections of lots of wind turbines. Wind farms are usually built in windy places such as mountaintops or plains. Sometimes they are built in the ocean. These are offshore wind farms.

This wind farm in California is one of the largest onshore wind farms in the world. It has at least six hundred turbines.

Planet Power

Another source of renewable energy is moving water, or hydropower. *Hydro* is Greek for "water."

Hydroelectric power plants are built on or near swiftly flowing rivers or big waterfalls. The moving water turns blades in a turbine, making electricity. Every state uses hydropower, although most big hydroelectric power plants are in California, Oregon, and Washington.

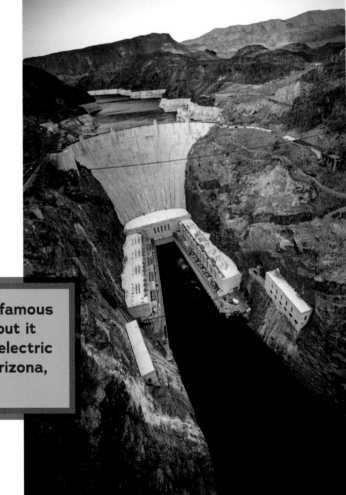

The Hoover Dam is a famous tourist attraction, but it also generates hydroelectric power for Nevada, Arizona, and California.

This geothermal power plant in Iceland created the famous Blue Lagoon geothermal spa. People come from all over to swim in the mineral-rich water that bubbles to the surface.

Earth also has energy within it, or heat under the ground. This geothermal energy is another type of renewable energy. The word *geothermal* comes from Greek words that mean "heat from Earth."

Geothermal power plants turn Earth's heat into electricity. Wells are drilled deep in the ground, and hot water or steam is pumped to the surface. The hot water or steam is then used to make electricity.

STEM In Depth: How Solar Panels Work

Solar panels are made of many solar cells. Each solar cell contains silicon, a substance found in sand. When sunlight strikes silicon in a solar cell, the energy from the sunlight is turned into electricity. The electricity flows through the electric lines and into your home.

Chapter 3

ENERGY-SMART INVENTIONS

How did you use energy today? Maybe you took a hot shower, played a video game, or rode in a car. Since most of our energy comes from fossil fuels, using energy contributes to climate change. Part of the problem with energy is that we use too much of it. But we could use less.

Recycling and unplugging machines saves energy. Scientists and engineers are also finding new approaches to save energy. They are working on energy-saving inventions.

Scientists are always looking for new approaches to our energy use. They are researching more efficient ways to use energy as well as alternative energy sources.

Go Green!

Some buildings, called green buildings, use much less energy than other buildings. These buildings may use natural sunlight for heat and light. They may have energy-efficient lights and appliances. They may have sensors that turn off lights and electronics when people are not in the room. They may collect rainwater from the roof or have systems for filtering and reusing wastewater.

Entire communities have been designed and built to make as much energy as they use, like this one in California.

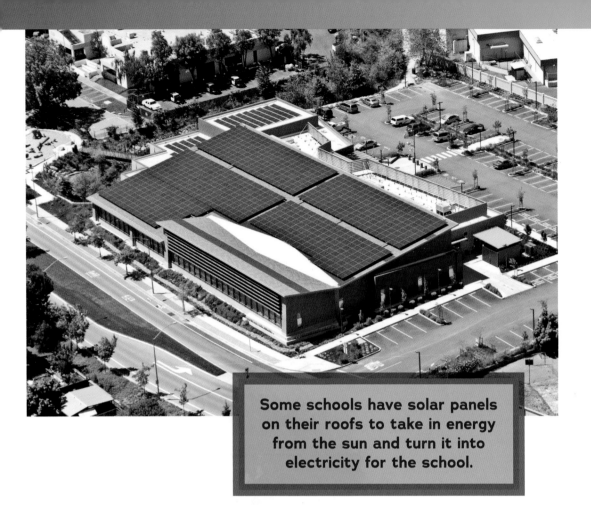

Some schools have solar panels on their roofs to take in energy from the sun and turn it into electricity for the school.

Some buildings can even make their own electricity. A rooftop may have solar panels or a row of small wind turbines.

Some green buildings use geothermal heating and cooling. In this system, pipes run 4 feet (1.2 m) or more underground, where the temperature stays about 55°F (13°C) all year. Heat pumps transfer geothermal heat into the building to warm it in winter. The process is reversed in summer, keeping the building cool.

Green Machines

Engineers are also building more efficient cars and trucks. Most cars and trucks in the United States run on gasoline, a fuel made from oil. Burning gasoline releases carbon dioxide into the air and contributes to climate change. But newer cars and trucks are more efficient. They use less fuel and create less pollution.

This car runs on electricity.

MANY ELECTRIC CARS USE CHARGING STATIONS TO RECHARGE THEIR BATTERIES.

One type of efficient vehicle is an electric car. It runs on electricity instead of gasoline. It uses an electric motor powered by a rechargeable battery. The owner can plug the car into an electrical outlet or a charging station to recharge the battery. If the electricity comes from renewable sources, the car doesn't cause pollution.

Another efficient vehicle is a hybrid car. A hybrid car is a cross between a gasoline-powered car and an electric car. It is more efficient and creates less pollution than a car powered only by gasoline.

Chapter 4

ENERGIZING THE FUTURE

How we make and use energy is strongly connected to climate change. So scientists and engineers around the world are developing new ways to harness energy without harming Earth. They are working hard to solve our energy problems.

Some engineers design and plan solar energy projects that provide energy for cities, businesses, and homes.

Researchers are testing solar batteries that last longer and save more energy from the sun.

Better Batteries

Around the world, researchers are working to build better batteries. The ones we have don't store a lot of energy. Improved batteries could power electric cars, trucks, and buses. Then the vehicles can go farther on a single charge. Better batteries also help make wind and solar power more reliable. The batteries can store extra energy on windy and sunny days. We can still use the batteries for electricity on cloudy, windless days.

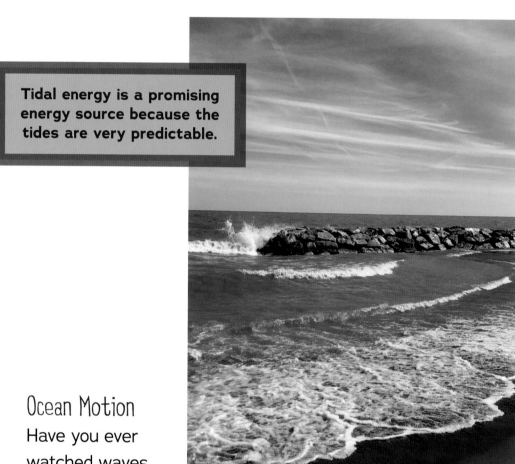

Tidal energy is a promising energy source because the tides are very predictable.

Ocean Motion

Have you ever watched waves on the ocean? Wind blowing across the surface of the water creates the waves. Those waves have energy.

Tides also have energy. The pull of the moon's gravity on the oceans creates tides. As Earth rotates, the oceans rise and fall in response to the moon's pull. This creates a cycle of two high tides and two low tides along coastlines on most days.

This wave energy device near the coast of Portugal uses floating tubes that bob in the ocean to pump fluid that drives generators.

Scientists and engineers are figuring out how to capture the energy of waves and tides. To capture wave energy, the waves are channeled into a basin. There the water can spin a turbine on the ocean floor. The turbine connects to a generator that makes electricity. Other wave energy devices float right on top of the water.

The western coasts of the United States and Europe and the coasts of New Zealand and Japan could be used to capture wave energy.

Tidal turbines turned by ocean currents can capture tidal energy. The turbines are placed in a narrow channel. When the tide comes in, water rises on one side of the channel. The water pours through the channel to the other side and turns the blades of the turbine. When the tide goes out, the water on the higher side flows back through the channel in reverse.

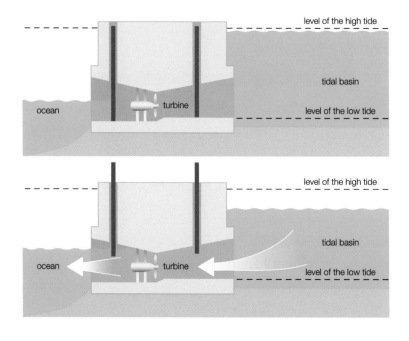

The best places to capture tidal energy are narrow channels of water between two landmasses. Tidal turbines should be close to where people live. One tidal turbine is being placed off the coast of Scotland. It is capable of making enough electricity to power one thousand homes.

Advances in energy technology are happening every day. One day, we may be able to use electricity completely created from renewable resources. Meanwhile, we all can do our part to save energy. Turning off lights, unplugging devices, and using less water will all help to combat climate change.

We can all do our part to help Earth!

What You Can Do

- **Carry reusable bags when you go shopping instead of using paper or plastic bags.** Plastic bags are made from petroleum, a fossil fuel product. Paper bags are made from trees, which absorb carbon dioxide from the air.

- **Drink from a reusable water bottle.** When people throw plastic water bottles away, they release methane, a heat-trapping gas that contributes to climate change.

- **Open your blinds or curtains on sunny winter days.** Let the sun warm the inside of your home to reduce the use of electricity.

- **Bike or walk short distances instead of asking for a ride in a car.** Biking and walking don't burn fossil fuels, so they release less carbon dioxide.

Climate Change Timeline

1760 The Industrial Revolution begins in Britain and spreads around the world, increasing the atmosphere's carbon dioxide levels.

1859 Irish scientist John Tyndall discovers that carbon dioxide traps heat from the sun. He realizes this gas can warm the planet.

1954 Three scientists working at Bell Labs invent the solar cell. It uses sunlight to power electrical machines.

1980 The world's first wind farm, with twenty wind turbines, opens in New Hampshire.

2007 Scientists with the Intergovernmental Panel on Climate Change blame climate change on human activities, including the burning of fossil fuels.

2013 Ivanpah, the world's largest solar thermal plant, opens. It makes enough electricity to power 140,000 California homes.

2016 Almost every nation on Earth signs the Paris Climate Agreement that will reduce greenhouse gas emissions.

Glossary

atmosphere: the layer of air that surrounds Earth

carbon dioxide: an invisible gas. Burning fossil fuels is one of the ways it is released into the air.

drought: a long dry period when an area does not receive enough rain

energy-efficient: capable of producing results while using less energy

fossil fuel: a fuel formed from the ancient remains of plants or animals

generator: a machine that uses the energy of motion to produce electricity

pollution: harmful waste made by humans and released into the environment

renewable: capable of being replaced naturally

turbine: a machine with blades that spin when pushed by water, steam, or air

Learn More about Energy Technology

Books

Green, Dan. *Eyewitness Energy.* New York: DK, 2016. Learn more about the energy that powers our world.

Hirsch, Rebecca E. *Birds vs. Blades? Offshore Wind Power and the Race to Protect Seabirds.* Minneapolis: Millbrook Press, 2017. Follow along as scientists track seabirds to learn about their movements and ensure offshore wind power won't harm birds.

Sneideman, Joshua, and Erin Twamley. *Renewable Energy: Discover the Fuel of the Future with 20 Projects.* White River Junction, VT: Nomad, 2016. Learn more about renewable energy sources and do hands-on projects.

Websites

Alliant Energy Kids
http://www.alliantenergykids.com
Play games, learn energy basics, and explore different types of renewable energy.

Energy Information Administration: Energy Kids
https://www.eia.gov/kids/
Explore all sorts of energy-related topics with games, timelines, and activities.

NASA: Climate Kids
https://climatekids.nasa.gov
This site from NASA has activities, games, and answers to your questions about climate change and energy.

Index

Photo Acknowledgments

Image credits: ND700/Shutterstock.com, p. 4; DeAgostini/Getty Images, p. 5; Oleksandra Petrovska/Shutterstock.com, p. 6; Jami Tarris/Minden Pictures/Getty Images, p. 7; Hans Blossey/imageBROKER/Getty Images, p. 8; Trum Ronnarong/Shutterstock.com, p. 9; Westend61/Getty Images, p. 10; ALFREDO ESTRELLA/AFP/Getty Images, p. 11; Miguel Navarro/Getty Images, p. 12; ChuckSchugPhotography/Getty Images, p. 13; JOE KLAMAR/AFP/Getty Images, p. 14; San Rostro/age fotostock/Getty Images, p. 15; Smit/Shutterstock.com, p. 16; Javier Larrea/age fotostock/Getty Images, p. 17; Billy Hustace/Corbis Documentary/Getty Images, p. 18; Steve Proehl/Corbis Documentary/Getty Images, p. 19; Michael H/DigitalVision/Getty Images, p. 20; sungsu han/Shutterstock.com, p. 21; ISAAC KASAMANI/AFP/Getty Images, p. 22; Golden Productions/age fotostock/Getty Images, p. 23; Judith Salstone/Shutterstock.com, p. 24; JOAO ABREU MIRANDA/AFP/Getty Images, p. 25; Encyclopaedia Britannica/UIG/Universal Images Group/Getty Images, p. 26; Emma Gibbs/Moment Open/Getty Images, p. 27.

Cover: Westend61/Getty Images.